Pour it on Jesus

Breaking
Your Alabaster Box

ISBN: 979-8-9917801-8-6

Dr. Tom Sexton

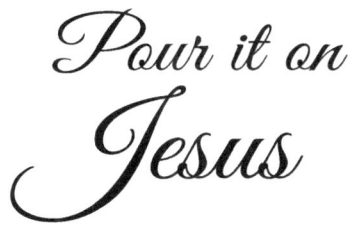

Breaking Your Alabaster Box

"Break Your Alabaster Box Sunday" will work if everyone gets on board and becomes consumed with doing something big for the LORD.

On our first "Break Your Alabaster Box Sunday" people gave money, a car, a house, two building sites, gold, jewels, etc. When it was all said and done, we received the largest offering in our ministry's history. Everyone wanted to have a part in it.

I shared the idea with a few of my pastor friends and they've had good success. Many have asked if I would make it available to others who were trying to raise funds.

If you allow each teacher to have their own copy of this book to read, they will be more effective in teaching the lessons. You may also want to use the book:

"Giving God's Way"
The golden key to the storehouse of blessings,
also published by Five Star Christian Ministries.

May God open the windows of Heaven and pour you out a blessing as you "Pour It on Jesus."

Your friend,

Tom Sexton Jr. 8:39

www.FiveStarChristianMinistries.com

TABLE OF CONTENTS

Breaking Your Alabaster Box.. 1

SECTION TWO   29

Song "Pour It On Jesus"...................................... 31

Introduction To Lessons..................................... 32

Lesson 1, Mary's Reason...................................... 33

Lesson 2, The Crowd's Reaction............................ 39

Lesson 3, The Lord's Response.............................. 44

Lesson 4, Mary's Reward...................................... 50

SECTION THREE   59

Student Outlines & Song Hand-Out.................... 60

Getting The Most Out Of This Campaign.......... 71

Are You Going To Heaven................................. 73

BREAKING THE ALABASTER BOX
Introduction

The Lord Jesus is coming to the close of His earthly mission, He is "in Bethany in the house of Simon the leper. As He sat at meat, there came a woman having an alabaster box of ointment of spikenard very precious; and she brake the box and poured it on His head.

And there were some that had indignation within themselves, and said, Why was this waste of the ointment made? For it might have been sold for more than three hundred pence, and have been given to the poor. And they murmured against her." This is Judas' first recorded words, and he is murmuring against what Mary has done for Jesus.

"And Jesus said, Let her alone; why trouble ye her? she hath wrought a good work on me. For ye have the poor with you always, and whensoever ye will ye may do them good: but Me ye have not always.

She hath done what she could: she is come aforehand to anoint My body to the burying. Verily I say unto you, Wheresoever this gospel shall be preached throughout the whole world, this also that she hath done shall be spoken of for a memorial of her." (1)

★ ★ ★ ★ ★

This event took place during the last week of our LORD's earthly ministry. But what make this so unusual is what Jesus said about what Mary did. This is the first and only time in the Bible where Jesus tells His followers to tell what someone has done for Him.

In the Gospels we read where Jesus tells those who have been healed, to "Go home to thy friends, and tell them how great things the Lord hath done for thee, and hath had compassion on thee." (2) But here Jesus tells everyone to go tell what Mary has done for him. Amazing!

God put in Mary's heart to do this for Jesus. God put something in Mary's heart to do for Jesus, and she did it!

Jesus tells His followers to tell the world and every generation what this woman has done for Him. As you may have figured out there is something very powerful about this act of love and kindness.

God puts His will and what He wants done on earth in the hearts of His children.

I have always stopped and listened very carefully when a Christian says, "God has put something in my heart to do for the Lord." I understand God puts everything He wants done in this world into the hearts of His followers.

I have given my life to help practicing Christians do what God has put in their heart to do. The question I have for you

★ ★ ★ ★ ★

is, What has God put in your heart to do with your life and treasures for Him?

May I quote a famous missionary who said,
            "Only one Life 'Twill soon be past.
            Only what's done For Christ will Last."
            Missionary C. T. Studd 1860-1931.

The Lord Jesus is trying to prepare His followers for His impending death. In a few days He would be crucified. He spoke to them on various occasions about this.

The first time He mentioned going to Calvary to die, Simon Peter rebuked Him; and for that, the LORD Jesus said to him, "Get thee behind Me, Satan" (3)

Ever since I first read that statement, I've been suspicious about those who say to me, "I'm behind you." I tell them to be careful that's where the devil is, and I don't want you back there with him, he will try to recruit you on his team. I want you here beside me where everyone knows what team you are on.

On that first occasion, He could not teach them great truth. Then on another occasion He talked about Calvary, and James and John, via their mother, asked for the best seats in the kingdom.

She said to Jesus, "Grant that these my two sons may sit, the one on Thy right hand, and the other on the left, in Thy kingdom. But Jesus answered and said, Ye know not what ye ask." (4)

★ ★ ★ ★ ★

But now Jesus is at Simon the leper's house in Bethany. This was an unusual place for Him to be. Simon is cleansed and home with his family, and he is holding a feast. Sitting at the table with the LORD Jesus is not just Simon the leper but "Lazarus…which had been dead, whom He raised from the dead." (5)

Wouldn't that have been something to see? Both the cleansed leper and the resurrected Lazarus were sitting with Jesus and enjoying fellowship with each other.

Then "Mary…anointed the feet of Jesus, and wiped His feet with her hair: and the house was filled with the odour of the ointment" (6) What a night! Mary did something that God mightily used because she was willing to break her alabaster box. I want you to think about breaking your alabaster box.

Nothing ever gets done for God without somebody breaking their alabaster box and taking care of what needs to be done.

The Bible says Jesus "went throughout every city and village, preaching and shewing the glad tidings of the kingdom of God: and the twelve were with Him, And certain women, which had been healed of evil spirits and infirmities, Mary called Magdalene, out of whom went seven devils,

And Joanna the wife of Chuza Herod's steward, and Susanna, and many others, which <u>ministered unto Him of their substance</u>." (7)

These followers who "ministered unto Him of their substance" made it possible for the LORD Jesus to do something in Galilee.

God is always looking for those who will break their alabaster box and do great and mighty things for God with their lives.

---

(1) Mark 14:3-9. (2) Mark 5:19. (3) Mark 8:33. (4) Matthew 20:21, 22. (5) John 12:1. (6) John 12:3. (7) Luke 8:1-3.

★ ★ ★ ★ ★

Chapter One
MARY'S REASON FOR DOING IT

Why did Mary break her alabaster box? The ointment, inside the alabaster box, was worth at that time almost a year's salary for a man and possibly three years' salary for a woman. Why would Mary take this expensive ointment and pour it on Jesus?

First, Because of Her Love For Jesus

She did it because she loved Jesus and because of what He had done for her. The LORD had allowed a tragedy to come into the lives of Mary; her brother, Lazarus; and her sister, Martha.

Lazarus became so ill that there was nothing that the doctors could do to help him; so, Mary and Martha sent for Jesus.

"When He [Jesus] had heard therefore that he was sick, He abode two days still in the same place where He was." (1)

Jesus delayed His going to see Lazarus, and finally Lazarus died. That's a hard thing to understand if you are Mary and Martha waiting on the LORD.

Have you ever had the LORD delay His coming in your life? Has something come into your life that was so serious and needful that you couldn't fix it; and when you prayed, nothing happened; it seemed as if Heaven were closed? Have you ever been disappointed with the way the LORD worked in your life?

★ ★ ★ ★ ★

We've all experienced God's delays, and we question what He is doing. But God had a plan and a purpose in Lazarus' sickness and his death.

When the LORD Jesus came, He spoke to Martha first. Mary was still inside the house. She knew the LORD Jesus was there, but in her heart, something was not right. Martha called her and said, "The Master has come, and calleth for thee." (2)

One of the reasons that the LORD Jesus delayed His coming to Mary and Martha's house was that He was trying to work in Mary's life. I thank God that there was a time when He brought some things into my life that I could not fix myself. I thank God that there was a day in my life when the Master came and 'called for me.'

I am glad that there was a day when I saw the need of Jesus Christ in my life; when I realized that I was a lost sinner on my way to a Devil's Hell; when I heard the good news of the Gospel and I turned my life over to Christ and trusted Him as my personal Savior. I thank God that I am now saved and on my way to Heaven.

If you have ever had God work in your life to get you to the place where you surrendered to Him, then you can understand why the LORD worked this way in Mary's life.

Mary loved Jesus for what He had done in her life. Aren't you glad that He still works in our lives? Aren't you glad that He stops us and gets our attention? If He didn't work in

★ ★ ★ ★ ★

circumstances in our lives, sometimes we would be far away from what He wants us to do.

He is as much in disturbances and circumstances as He is in deliverances.

One of my favorite verses is Psalm 143:8: "Cause me to hear Thy lovingkindness in the morning; for in Thee do I trust: cause me to know the way wherein I should walk; for I lift up my soul unto Thee."

Dear Friend, there are times when the LORD brings things into our lives to get our attention, and that's how He was working in Mary's life. He got her attention and then changed the direction of her life. "The Master is come, and calleth for thee." (3)

Maybe you are now going through some things in your life, and you wonder what is happening. Maybe the LORD is trying to get your attention.

Second, For What Jesus Did For Her Family

Another reason Mary broke her alabaster box was because of what Christ had done for her family. Her brother had gotten so sick that he had died—you can't get any worse than that—and they buried him.

When the LORD Jesus came, Mary said, "Lord, if thou hadst been here, my brother had not died." (4)

Jesus reminded her, "I am the resurrection, and the life: he that believeth in Me, though he were dead, yet shall he live." (5)

Then Jesus went to the grave of Lazarus. "He cried with a loud voice, Lazarus, come forth.

And he that was dead came forth, bound hand and foot with graveclothes: and his face was bound about with a napkin. Jesus saith unto them, Loose him, and let him go." (6)

I like what the old preacher said, that if the LORD Jesus had not called Lazarus by name, every person who had ever died would have come back to life because of the power of His Word.

What a day that was when God brought Mary's brother back to life!

I thank God for what He has brought into my life. Can you imagine God's saving a teenage boy named Clarence Sexton; then calling him to preach; then saving his brother, Tom Sexton; and their mother and sisters and then their "Pop"?

How good God is to do that for the Sexton family! What a Saviour we have!

We ought to love Him enough to break our alabaster box because of what He has done for us and what He has done for our families. Whole families are on their way to Heaven because of what the LORD has done for them!

★ ★ ★ ★ ★

God can save your whole household.

The apostle Paul and Silas gave this testimony to the jailer when he asked, "Sirs, what must I do to be saved?

And they said, Believe on the Lord Jesus Christ, and thou shalt be saved, and thy house." (7)

If your family is not saved, you ought to get serious about getting them saved and claim this promise of God that Paul gave to the jailer. Paul could make that statement with conviction because before he got saved, he had family members who were already saved.

Paul said, "Salute Andronicus and Junia, my kinsmen, and my fellow prisoners, who are of note among the apostles, who also were in Christ before me." (8) Paul's sister prayed that God might save her brother.

At that time, he was called Saul, and he was a tough case. It wasn't easy to get his attention. So, she prayed and asked God to do something, and God reached down on the road to Damascus, got Saul's attention, turned his life around, saved him, and then used him mightily.

Later, this same sister's son "heard of their lying-in wait [to kill his uncle Paul, and] he went and entered into the castle, and told Paul." (9)

No wonder Paul could say with certainty, "Believe on the Lord Jesus Christ, and thou shalt be saved, and thy house"!

★ ★ ★ ★ ★

We need to seize the opportunity to see our family and friends come to know the LORD. We ought to become desperate about our unsaved family members and become desperate about asking God to work in their lives. Our father died when we were young, and my mother was widowed with four children.

My father had lived a hard life and suffered greatly in his final days of life, spending them in a care facility similar to our nursing homes or Hope Hospice.

Several years after my brother Clarence had been preaching, a dear preacher came up to him and said that he used to go to a place on Sunday afternoons and hold services. He told my brother that he had met a man and thought because his last name was Sexton he might have been related to us.

When he told my brother that the man's name was Preston Sexton, my brother said, "That was my father." This dear preacher informed him that our father had trusted Christ as his personal Saviour in the final days of his life and had shown a real interest in the things of God.

Thank God for those who give their time to help people in nursing homes to know Christ. Imagine God saving my father and then my brother hearing about it years after he'd been preaching. I rejoice when people get saved in our church, and we work hard at soul winning.

We had a teenage girl get saved, and she began praying for her father to get saved. He had left her mother and had been

★ ★ ★ ★ ★

gone for three months, but God got ahold of his heart, and he got saved. God brought him back home to his family. It should thrill our hearts when we see families getting saved.

Thirdly, For What Jesus Had Done for Her Friends

"Then many of the Jews which came to Mary, and had seen the things which Jesus did, believed on Him." (10) God got their attention!

Before Lazarus' death, can't you picture Mary, Martha, and Lazarus telling their neighbors what God had done in their lives, telling them about the LORD Jesus and pleading with them to trust the LORD.

But they rejected what was told to them until one day God brought something into all their lives with which they could not deal, something that only God could fix.

Jesus delayed His coming long enough to get everybody's attention; and then, because His timing was perfect, the LORD Jesus came and not only brought Lazarus back from the dead, but He also saved their friends in Bethany.

And God is still able to save! "Whosoever shall call upon the name of the Lord shall be saved." (11) Mary started thinking about what God had done for her and her family and what He had done in her neighborhood and among her friends, and she could not help but love Jesus.

★ ★ ★ ★ ★

The Holy Spirit put something in her heart to do, she came and broke this alabaster box full of ointment. She didn't take off the lid and pour out just a little; she broke it and poured every drop over the LORD Jesus.

If you know the Savior; if you know that you are going to Heaven; if you know that you are not going to spend eternity in a Devil's Hell; if you have had the joy and privilege of seeing your loved ones come to Christ; if you have seen God work in the lives of people you know and love, then, dear Friend, you have a reason to break the alabaster box at the LORD Jesus' feet!

(1) John 11:6 (2) John 11:28. (3) John 11:28. (4) John 11:32. (5) John 11:25. (6) John 11:43,44. (7) Acts 16:30,31. (8) Romans 16:7. (9) Acts 23:16. (10) John 11:45. (11) Romans 10:13.

★ ★ ★ ★ ★

Chapter Two
THE CROWD'S REACTION

What was the crowd's reaction? It is amazing what they said. In fact, in the three Gospels where this story is told, we get the reactions of three different groups of people.

The "Do Nothing" Crowd

These are those who thought it should not have been done.

"Then saith one of His disciples, Judas Iscariot, Simon's son, which should betray Him,

Why was not this ointment sold for three hundred pence, and given to the poor?

This he said, not that he cared for the poor; but because he was a thief, and had the bag, and bare what was put therein." (1)

We should not be surprised at Judas Iscariot's reaction, nor should we be surprised that there is a Judas crowd around today. In fact, you must climb over them to do anything.

Every time you get excited about God, every time you start to do something for Him, the Judas crowd won't like it at all. In fact, they don't think anything should ever be done for the LORD Jesus.

They think it is terrible when Christians give up a Wednesday night to go to church in the middle of the week instead of playing ball with the team. They think it is crazy to give money or time to a ministry. This crowd doesn't want anything done.

The "Measure and Pour" Crowd

These are the ones who thought it should have been measured out, not poured out.

"Now when Jesus was in Bethany, in the house of Simon the leper,

There came unto Him a woman having an alabaster box of very precious ointment, and poured it on His head, as He sat at meat.

But when His disciples saw it, they had indignation, saying, To what purpose is this waste?" (2) The disciples didn't mind Mary's pouring ointment on the LORD Jesus, but they thought she got carried away with it.

They thought she was a little too crazy about it. Why not use just a little bit? Why waste it all on Him?

That's the crowd that puts in exactly what their tithe is and that's it - not one penny beyond that amount.

When you say, 'Show up on Sunday morning, Sunday night, Wednesday night, and visitation night,' they will ask, 'How many hours do you want from us, Preacher?'

★ ★ ★ ★ ★

This crowd will measure out their lives until the trumpet sounds, and this crowd has never done anything great for God! They will take off the alabaster box lid, but they'll only pour out what is absolutely necessary.

They don't understand what Mary saw or what she got ahold of. This crowd is filled with indignation.

The "Turn Loose and Pour It on Jesus" Crowd

These are those who believe it should be poured on Jesus. "[They] sat at the table with Him." (3)

The crowd that gets it done is the crowd that breaks the alabaster box, the crowd that turns loose of it all and pours it on the LORD Jesus.

One of those sitting at the table was Simon the leper. He'd been cleansed; he was at home with his family; he was enjoying the sweet fellowship of family and friends and especially the LORD Jesus.

If it were not for the LORD Jesus, he would be in a place for lepers, separated for the rest of his life. If he were to comment, he would say, Break it! Break it! Pour it all on Jesus!'

Lazarus, who had been dead, also sat with Jesus. If it were not for the LORD Jesus, he would be lying in some cold grave. If he had spoken up, he would have said, 'Mary, give it all to Jesus!'

★ ★ ★ ★ ★

Those who have been touched by God, those who have been brought back to life, those who have been "quickened, who were dead in trespasses and sins" (4) They are part of this crowd. They say, 'Pour it all on Jesus!'

If there was ever a time in your life when you needed the blood of Jesus to cleanse your heart, and every child of God needs that, - then you ought to be a part of this crowd.

Every Christian is a part of one of these three crowds: the Judas crowd, the indignant crowd, or the break-the-alabaster-box crowd.

There is nothing that should be held back from Jesus. We need to pour it all out on the LORD.

Through all of this - Mary's action and the reactions of Judas and the disciples - Jesus had been silent. He was just sitting there. Remember, He had been trying to prepare His disciples for what lay ahead.

He had tried to tell them about Calvary and His death before, but Simon Peter rebuked Him. When He tried to tell them again, James and John, by way of their mother, tried to get the best seats in the kingdom.

He must have been wondering how to get their attention on what He wanted to tell them.

---

(1) John 12:4-6. (2) Matthew 26:6-8. (3) John 12:2. (4) Ephesians 2:1.

★ ★ ★ ★ ★

Chapter Three
THE LORD'S RESPONSE TO MARY'S GIFT

What was the LORD Jesus' reaction? There is an interesting statement in Matthew 26:10 that makes you stop and meditate: "When Jesus understood it...."

He was sitting there as the crowds reacted to Mary's action. Judas made his first comment recorded in the Bible, and the disciples let their opinion be known. Simon the leper and Lazarus, who had been dead, were sitting at the table with Jesus, watching Him as they smelled this ointment and saw Mary wipe His feet with her hair.

Throughout all of this, the LORD Jesus was silent. And then the Word of God says, "When Jesus understood it...."

In other words, God revealed it to Him, and He understood it. He understood that God had found someone who had such a love for the LORD Jesus and wanted so much to do something for God that God put this inside her heart. Look at what Jesus did when 'He understood it.'

He Accepted It

The LORD Jesus accepted it. "And Jesus said, Let her alone; why trouble ye her? she hath wrought a good work on Me." (1)

The goal of Christians ought to be to please God, to be acceptable to Him, pleasing Him with our lives, doing what He wants us to do.

★ ★ ★ ★ ★

"Let the words of my mouth, and the meditation of my heart, be <u>acceptable in Thy sight</u>, O Lord, my strength, and my redeemer." (2)

"I beseech you therefore, brethren, by the mercies of God, that ye present your bodies a living sacrifice, holy, <u>acceptable unto God</u>, which is your reasonable service.

And be not conformed to this world: but be ye transformed by the renewing of your mind, that ye may prove what is that good, and <u>acceptable</u>, and perfect, will of God." (3)

Are we living a life that is acceptable to the LORD? The highest goal of Christian living is to please the LORD. The LORD Jesus, who is our example said, "I do always those things that please Him." (4)

He Appraised It

The LORD Jesus appraised it. "She hath done what she could: she is come aforehand to anoint My body to the burying." (5)

It was worth something, and He put this price tag on it. Mary had done it all. There was nothing else she could have done.

Don't you want to meet the LORD someday and hear Him say, "You have done what you could"?

Each one of us is given different abilities, different talents, and different things we can do.

★ ★ ★ ★ ★

We have different measures of faith, but it is wonderful to come across a child of God who takes what God has given them and puts it all on the altar. One day that person will hear the LORD Jesus say, "You have done what you could."

I want to take advantage of the opportunities that God has given me; I want to do with my life all that can be accomplished in my life. That's the way Mary felt. She wanted to do something for God with her life, and the LORD Jesus said, "Let her alone; why trouble ye her? she hath wrought a good work on Me."

She hath done what she could: she is come aforehand to anoint My body to the burying." (6) After accepting it and appraising it, Jesus did something else.

He Anointed It and Used It

The LORD Jesus anointed it and used it. "Verily I say unto you, Wheresoever this gospel shall be preached in the whole world, there shall also this, that this woman hath done, be told for a memorial of her." (7)

I've always been amazed at what God revealed to women in the Bible and how He used them in a mighty way - here is one of them! While Judas was whining about the loss of income from Mary's act; while the disciples were wondering how things were going to work out for them, Mary was waiting on God.

Mary saw what others could not see. As she looked at the LORD Jesus sitting at the table with Lazarus and Simon, she saw what Christ came to do.

On one side are those who are dead in trespasses and sin. On the other side are those who are unclean because of sin. God put it in her heart to break the box and pour the ointment because it is a picture of what was going to happen on Calvary.

The LORD Jesus was going to shed His blood on Calvary. Calvary is not a waste. Calvary is not God's measuring a little. Calvary is where Christ was broken and poured out for those who are dead in trespasses and sins, and for those who are unclean because of sin.

God put this in Mary's heart and the LORD Jesus understood that this object lesson could be used to help others understand what Calvary is all about.

As soon as the LORD put it in her heart, she ran and grabbed up her alabaster box, went back to the table, walked past Judas and the disciples, broke her alabaster box, and poured all its contents over Jesus. Then she knelt on her hands and knees and wiped His feet with her hair.

God has the power to give life to those who are dead in trespasses, and the blood of Jesus cleanses us from sin. No one is so far gone that God cannot save him, or so far away from Him that He can't cleanse his heart.

★ ★ ★ ★ ★

Mary didn't pour the ointment from the box; she broke the box and poured all of it on Him, and the Bible says that "Jesus understood it."

He realized that Mary saw Calvary and that she understood that Calvary was not a waste; it would be the place of salvation, the place of cleansing. She saw that enough blood would be shed on Calvary to reach the world and that the cleansing blood of Jesus would wash away our sin. Nobody else saw that, not even His disciples; and when Jesus understood that, He anointed it and taught a great lesson.

"When Jesus understood it, He said unto them, Why trouble ye the woman? for she hath wrought a good work upon Me.

For ye have the poor always with you; but Me ye have not always. For in that she hath poured this ointment on My body, she did it for My burial.

Verily I say unto you, Wheresoever this gospel shall be preached in the whole world, there shall also this, that this woman hath done, be told for a memorial of her." (8)

This helps us to understand the Gospel. The LORD Jesus was able to anoint this act and use it in such a mighty way that for nearly two thousand years this act of love and kindness and dedication has been used to stir the hearts of people to come to Jesus. It has been used to stir the hearts of God's people to break their alabaster boxes at the feet of Jesus and pour it all on the LORD.

---

(1) Mark 14:6. (2) Psalms. 19:14. (3) Romans 12:1,2. (4) John 8:29. (5) Mark 14:8. (6) Mark 14:6,8. (7) Matthew 26:13. (8) Matthew 26:10-13.

★ ★ ★ ★ ★

Chapter Four
MARY'S REWARD

What was Mary's reward? The LORD said, "Tell it! Tell this story!" That's what I'm doing now because He wants us to see Mary's reward. I don't know what it will be like, but I know this: it is going to be exciting!

Can you imagine that one of these days - and I believe it will be soon - the LORD is coming? This generation of Christians is closer to the LORD's coming than any other generation that has ever lived! That ought to excite you!

"For the Lord Himself shall descend from heaven with a shout, with the voice of the archangel, and with the trump of God: and the dead in Christ shall rise first:

Then we which are alive and remain, shall be caught up together with them in the clouds, to meet the Lord in the air: and so shall we ever be with the Lord.

Wherefore comfort one another with these words." (1)

That "shout" is going to change the world! We're going to get a glorified body and have the mind of Christ. The last person saved is the first one to appear at the Judgment Seat of Christ, and then we will go all the way back to the first ones saved.

We're going to see all those who made it possible for us to read this message. I'm going to meet the man who went by

★ ★ ★ ★ ★

a nursing home facility and led my father to the LORD, and we had no idea that he had been saved.

We're going to see that man, and we'll see the ones who led him to Christ, and we'll work our way back to the disciples.

What a time that's going to be! No wonder the apostle Paul said, "Holding forth the word of life; that I may rejoice in the day of Christ, that I have not run in vain, neither laboured in vain" (2)

Imagine the celebration that we're going to have with a glorified body, and the mind of Christ, and the ability to understand all that took place down through the centuries in order for us to know Jesus! What a day of rejoicing that will be! Then we're going to meet Mary. I don't know what she did with the rest of her life.

As far as I know, she did not become a missionary, but 'she did all that she could' - she broke her alabaster box.

Then the LORD Jesus did something so kind and gracious: He challenged everybody who ever preaches the Gospel to tell the story. He loved her so much, and what she did was so powerful that He wanted every man who ever preached to 'tell this story as a memorial to her.'

What she did that day is not finished. Her act of kindness and dedication is still making an investment to this day.

Every time this story is mentioned, a reward is being stored up for her, and one of these days she'll receive her reward, and we'll see it. I cannot wait to see what God pours on this woman because of her one act of love for her Savior.

WILL YOU BREAK YOUR ALABASTER BOX?

This story reminds us that it is so important to do what God puts in our hearts to do. What we do has an effect and an influence on every generation to follow.

Somewhere a handful of people with an alabaster box made your church a reality. Every time that God has ever done anything, somebody has had to break an alabaster box.

Can you imagine what would get done in this world if everyone who is saved would, with a grateful heart, bring his alabaster box and break it for the LORD?

The truth of the matter is, many of us are like the disciples who were sitting there that day and not seeing what Mary saw. Mary saw more, she saw a bigger picture of Calvary.

What do you see? The LORD puts in the hearts of His people what He wants done. What has God put in your heart to do?

Years ago, we had a missionary give his testimony in our church. As a ten-year-old boy, he had surrendered at a camp

★ ★ ★ ★ ★

to become a missionary. When he was thirty years old, he was on the mission field in a village, and he met a man who had gotten saved twenty years prior to them meeting.

The man said, "The missionary that led me to the LORD knelt down beside me and my family and prayed that God would touch somebody's heart and that he would come to this village and be a missionary." Twenty years later he saw the answer to that prayer.

God heard those people praying, and He reached over and touched a ten-year-old child's heart, and he surrendered to become a missionary. That is the way the LORD works.

What is God doing in your life? Has He spoken to you about something? Has He put a desire in your heart to do something? There is something special you can do for God's work.

Will you break your alabaster box and pour it on the LORD Jesus? You'll be glad you did.

---

(1) I Thessalonians 4:16-18. (2) Philippians 2:16.

★ ★ ★ ★ ★

People Are Just People

People are just people, no matter the color of their skin.

At our best we are just people, flawed women and men.

Naked we're born with so much to learn,

At the end of our journey, naked we'll return.

Some make it big and others stay the same.

Some have great talent and achieve worldwide fame.

Some give their life to make all they can.

Some come to Christ and faithfully follow His plan.

Some make fortunes and have the world in their hands.

Some lift up Jesus the Saviour for every man.

Millions who were in darkness

Have been given new birth,

By the ones taking the Gospel to the ends of the earth.

Yes, people are just people no matter when they live,

But the ones who count are the ones who give.

★ ★ ★ ★ ★

Pour it on Jesus

★ ★ ★ ★ ★

SECTION TWO

Pour it on Jesus

Breaking
Your Alabaster Box

*Teaching This Great
Truth To Others*

★ ★ ★ ★ ★   29

Pour It On Jesus
Song

Teacher Lessons

MARY'S REASON FOR POURING IT ON JESUS

THE CROWD'S REACTION TO MARY'S GIFT

THE LORD'S RESPONSE TO MARY'S GIFT

MARY'S HEAVENLY REWARD

Dr. Tom Sexton

★ ★ ★ ★ ★

Pour It on Jesus
Sung to the tune of "Tell It To Jesus"

Have you trusted Christ's work of redemption?
Pour it on Jesus, pour it on Jesus.
Do you know Him as your Lord and Saviour?
Pour it on Jesus today.

CHORUS

Have you loved ones lost in their sin?
Pour it on Jesus, pour it on Jesus.
There's no other who can redeem them.
Pour it on Jesus today.

CHORUS

There are others waiting on the message.
Pour it on Jesus, pour it on Jesus.
The devil's kingdom can be defeated!
Pour it on Jesus today.

CHORUS

Do you long for treasures up in heaven?
Pour it on Jesus, pour it on Jesus.
Then you must make an investment.
Pour it on Jesus today.

CHORUS

Pour it on Jesus, pour it on Jesus.
There is no gift that's a waste.
He's our Saviour and He has redeemed us.
Pour it on Jesus today.

★ ★ ★ ★ ★

Introduction To Lessons
Matthew 26:6-13, Mark 14:3-9, John 12:2-11

It is the last week of the LORD's earthly ministry. He will soon be put to death. He is now in the shadow of the cross. On two occasions He has mentioned the nearness of the cross. The first time, Peter rebukes Him and is called Satan. The second time, two of His disciples ask (by way of their mother) if they can have the two highest seats of honor in His kingdom. They are now in Simon the leper's house, enjoying a time of fellowship and rejoicing over the victories concerning Lazarus and Simon.

Mary comes into the room with a very precious box of ointment. She goes straight to Jesus and, to everyone's amazement, breaks the box and begins to pour the oil on the LORD's head. Soon she is pouring the ointment on His feet and wiping them with her hair.

Shock fills the room. No one can believe what she has done. As the fragrance fills the room, people begin to react to what she has done. The LORD will take what she has done and teach a great truth that will one day change everyone's lives. As we look at this event we will see:
1. **Mary's Reason for Doing It**
2. **The Crowd's Reaction**
3. **The LORD's Response to Mary's Gift**
4. **Mary's Reward**

How often, in our lifetime, do we get to do something for the LORD Jesus? As we study these lessons and what happened in Simon the leper's house, may the LORD Jesus help us to "Break Our Alabaster Box" for Him.

★ ★ ★ ★ ★

Lesson #1
MARY'S REASON FOR POURING IT ON JESUS

"There they made Him a supper; and Martha served: but Lazarus was one of them that sat at the table with Him. Then took Mary a pound of ointment of spikenard, very costly, and anointed the feet of Jesus, and wiped His feet with her hair: and the house was filled with the odour of the ointment." John 12:2-11.

As we study this lesson, we must look at Mary's reasoning for doing what she did. Why do people do what they do? Someone has said that two of the greatest motives of life are love and money.

Many people do what they do because of a love for money, but Mary loved the Lord Jesus. Her motive was pure. It was love for Christ that compelled her to do it. Love told her the duty of the hour.

People who truly love Jesus think of ways to show it. Mary's love and devotion to Christ was based on three things. **Why did Mary break her alabaster box of ointment and pour it on Jesus?**

Mary Broke Her Alabaster Box
First, because of what Jesus had done for her.

"Jesus saith unto her, Said I not unto thee, that, if thou wouldest believe, thou shouldest see the glory of God…Salvation is of the LORD." John 11:40. "And you hath he quickened, who were dead in trespasses and sins;" Ephesians 2:1.

Mary knew the Lord Jesus as her personal Saviour. She was a believer. But when she sent for Jesus, He remained two days before He came to Bethany. Mary, like us, wanted the Lord to do something the moment she asked.

We all have a hard time waiting on the Lord. Waiting on the Lord is difficult, especially when we have an urgent request.

How many times have we asked God to help, and it was like our prayer fell to the ground. The Bible says, "Wait on the LORD: be of good courage, and he shall strengthen thine heart: wait, I say, on the LORD." Psalms 27:14.

Mary is going to discover there is a much bigger picture concerning her brother's healing than she sees.

Lazareth dying has shaken her faith. She did not come with Martha to meet Jesus outside the city. Perhaps she was disappointed with Jesus letting her brother Lazareth die. She may have even had a root of bitterness toward God.

What we do know is that Jesus is now calling her to come to Him. She is going to learn a great lesson about how God works through circumstances to bring people to Him.

Mary cannot see the big picture and now finds herself disappointed with God. I have had Christians tell me they were

★ ★ ★ ★ ★

having a hard time forgiving God because of His delays in answering their prayer.

The Bible says, "For my thoughts are not your thoughts, neither are your ways my ways, saith the LORD. For as the heavens are higher than the earth, so are my ways higher than your ways, and my thoughts than your thoughts." Isaiah 55:8-9.

Soon she will learn why all that happened in her family had a greater purpose. It was to bring them closer to God. She thought death was final. "Jesus said…I am the resurrection, and the life: he that believeth in Me, though he were dead, yet shall he live: And whosoever liveth and believeth in Me shall never die…" John 11:25-26.

God allows things to come into our lives not to discourage us, but to strengthen our faith.

Mary Broke Her Alabaster Box
Second, because of what Jesus has done for her family.

"And when he thus had spoken, he cried with a loud voice, <u>Lazarus, come forth</u>. And he that was dead came forth, bound hand and foot with graveclothes: and his face was bound about with a napkin. Jesus saith unto them, Loose him, and let him go." John 11:43-44.

Lazareth dying had shaken her faith. Mary had something come into her life that Jesus said would bring glory to God. She remembered what Jesus said when her and Martha sent

★ ★ ★ ★ ★   35

for Him when her brother was at deaths door. He said, This sickness is not unto death, but for the glory of God, that the Son of God might be glorified thereby." John 11:4.

Her family had been touched by heartache. Now her brother is dead. All hope is gone.

But Jesus said unto her, "Said I not unto thee, that, if thou wouldest believe, thou shouldest see the glory of God?" John 11:40.

Her faith is now tested. She believed and saw the Lord work. Mary has been transformed by what has taken place in her life.

There was nothing anyone else could do but to lay Lazarus in a grave.

When we come to the end of our resources, then the Lord can do what He can only do. Christ did for Mary's family what no one else could do. When we think of what Christ has done for our family, we should want to give to Him. Someone must believe if the Lord is going to do great and mighty things.

Jesus said, "if thou wouldest believe, thou shouldest see the glory of God." Have faith in God. Just believe and you will see.

The breaking of her alabaster box was her testimony that she can always trust God. The Bible says, "Trust in him at all times; ye people, pour out your heart before him: God is a refuge for us. Selah." Psalms 62:8.

What the Lord Jesus did in her life brought her to another level of love and dedication. She loved Jesus because of what He has done for her.

Loving Jesus is the greatest motive for serving the Lord.
The Bible says, "For the love of Christ constraineth us…" II Corinthians 5:14.

It is our love for Christ that will keep us going when all other motives fail. If someone truly loves Christ, they will find a way to show it. When we think of what Christ has done for us, we should want to give ourselves to Him.

Mary Broke Her Alabaster Box
Third, because of what Jesus has done for her friends and neighbors.

"Then <u>many of the Jews</u> which came to Mary, and had seen the things which Jesus did, <u>believed on him</u>." John 11:45.

Lazarus, Martha, and Mary loved their neighbors and friends, and wanted them to know Christ as their personal Saviour. Now they are at Mary and Martha's home comforting the two heartbroken sisters. It is for their salvation that the Lord has allowed this family to go through this valley.

The salvation of the lost is what shows us the "glory of God." Bethany will forever be known for the day Lazarus rose from the dead.

★ ★ ★ ★ ★

Questions to consider.

- How has the Lord strengthened your faith?

- How has God helped you see a bigger picture of what He is doing?

- Have you seen the Lord work in your friends and neighbor's lives?

★ ★ ★ ★ ★

Lesson #2

THE CROWD'S REACTION TO MARY'S UNUSUAL GIFT

"And being in Bethany in the house of Simon the leper, as He sat at meat, there came a woman having an alabaster box of ointment of spikenard very precious; and she break the box and poured it on His head. And there were some that had indignation within themselves, and said, Why was this waste of the ointment made? For it might have been sold for more than three hundred pence and have been given to the poor. And they murmured against her." Mark 14:3-9, vv. 3-5.

The Bible says that "...they murmured against her." As we read the other Gospel accounts of this event, we see there were three groups of people that had a reaction to her gift. These three groups represent the three groups that are in our churches. All of us will find ourselves in one of these three groups.

Some Thought Nothing Should Been Done

"Then saith one of His disciples, Judas Iscariot, Simon's son, which should betray Him, Why was not this ointment sold for three hundred pence, and given to the poor? This he said, not that he cared for the poor..." John 12:4-6.

Judas represents this group. He neither cared for the poor nor for Jesus. There seems to always be those who do not care for Christ, and the things of God, around people who want to pour out their lives to the Lord.

★ ★ ★ ★ ★

There are those who want no part in what is being done for Christ. They are like the ones we read about in the Old Testament who were told, "Shall your brethren go to war, and shall ye sit here?" Numbers 32:6.

The Bible records that Judas thought it should not have been done. There are those who get angry when anyone gives to Christ. Some in our churches fit in with this group. They have never given anything valuable to the work of the Lord.

It is sad to think that there are those who sit in our churches, and hear and see all that is happening, who never give in the offering, hand out a Gospel tract, or tell anyone about Christ.

Some Thought It Should Have Been Measured Out, Not Poured Out

"There came unto Him a woman having an alabaster box of very precious ointment, and poured it on His head…<u>But when His disciples saw it, they had indignation</u>, saying, To what purpose is this waste?" Matthew 26:7-8.

The other disciples represent this group. There are those who do not mind being measured out and giving a little, but don't want the box broken and poured out because then they look bad.

Some measure what they do for Christ. They believe, "the tenth shall be holy unto the LORD…" Leviticus 27:32.

They measure just what belongs to the Lord, and not a cent more.

"Will a man rob God? Yet ye have robbed Me. But ye say, Wherein have we robbed Thee? In tithes and offerings. Ye are cursed with a curse: for ye have robbed Me, even this whole nation.

Bring ye all the tithes into the storehouse, that there may be meat in Mine house, and prove Me now herewith, saith the LORD of hosts, if I will not open you the windows of heaven, and pour you out a blessing, that there shall not be room enough to receive it." Malachi 3:8-10.

The disciples' reaction was "to what purpose was this waste?"

In other words, they thought, 'It is okay to give a tenth, but don't overdo it.' (When they later understood the truth of Calvary, they had a change of heart.) There are those who only do what is required.

Some break and pour what they do for Christ. In the book of Acts, we read about many who "were possessors of lands or houses sold them and brought the prices of the things that were sold and laid them down at the apostles' feet…" Acts 4:34-35.

The disciples later became part of the group who pour it on Jesus. There will always be those who will do just what the Lord requires but will have a hard time doing more than a good measure.

★ ★ ★ ★ ★　　41

Some Believed It Should Be All Poured Out On Jesus

"And there were <u>some</u> that had indignation." Mark 14:4. Mark's Gospel says "some," not all. There were some who believed it should be poured out. There were at least two other people sitting at the table with Jesus. This group is represented by Simon, the person with leprosy, and Lazarus.

Simon, the Lord Jesus had cleansed this person of leprosy. The Bible says, "And being in Bethany in the house of Simon the leper, as He sat at meat." Mark 14:3,

Leprosy was a horrible disease that forced those who had it to a life of loneliness. Simon had been cleansed of leprosy by the Lord and could now enjoy the sweet fellowship of his family and friends. He would say, "Pour it on Jesus."

Lazarus had been brought back to life by the Lord Jesus "Then Jesus six days before the passover came to Bethany, where Lazarus was which had been dead, whom He raised from the dead...but Lazarus was one of them that sat at the table with Him." John 12:1-2.

Lazarus had been sick and had died. In his final days there would have been some weeping on the family's part. Death is something that has touched every family.

The Bible says, "But thanks be to God, which giveth us the victory through our Lord Jesus Christ." I Corinthians 15:57. Lazarus would have looked at his sister and said, "Pour it on Jesus."

　　　　★ ★ ★ ★ ★

Everyone will find themselves in one of these three groups. Anyone who understands the great gift that God gave will join the "Pour it on Jesus" group.

Questions to consider.

- Are there people in our churches who do nothing for the Lord? For example, they do not give, serve in the ministry, or invite others to church.

- Are there those in our churches who do only what is required? For example, they give exactly 10% to the penny in giving the tithe. They do the minimum in service or church attendance.

- Are there those in our churches who hold back nothing? In their giving and Christian service, they find ways to pour out their lives to Christ.

The big question is, "What group do you want to be in?"

★ ★ ★ ★ ★

Lesson #3
THE LORD'S RESPONSE TO MARY'S GIFT

"And being in Bethany in the house of Simon the leper, as He sat at meat, there came a woman having an alabaster box of ointment of spikenard very precious; and she brake the box, and poured it on His head. And there were some that had indignation within themselves, and said, Why was this waste of the ointment made? For it might have been sold for more than three hundred pence, and have been given to the poor. And they murmured against her.

<u>And Jesus said, Let her alone; why trouble ye her? she hath wrought a good work on Me.</u> For ye have the poor with you always, and whensoever ye will ye may do them good: but Me ye have not always. <u>She hath done what she could:</u> she is come aforehand to anoint My body to the burying.

Verily I say unto you, Wheresoever this gospel shall be preached throughout the whole world, this also that she hath done shall be spoken of for a memorial of her." Mark 14:3-9.

Picture in your mind the Lord Jesus sitting at a table with Simon the leper on one side and Lazarus which had been dead on the other side.

Mary comes straight to the Lord Jesus and begins to pour all this precious ointment over His head, and it flows down His face. Now she is on her knees wiping His feet with her hair.

The Lord Jesus is silent while Mary does what God put in her heart to do. The disciples have each had their reaction recorded, and now the Lord Jesus breaks His silence. Why trouble ye the woman? For ye have the poor always with you; but me ye have not always. For in that she hath poured this ointment on my body, she did it for my burial. Verily I say unto you, Wheresoever this gospel shall be preached in the whole world, there shall also this, that this woman hath done, be told for a memorial of her." Matthew 26:10-13.

What do we learn from Christ's response?

He Accepted It
Jesus said, "Let her alone…why trouble ye her…
She hath wrought a good work on Me." Mark 14:6.

The Lord Jesus accepted Mary's act of love and kindness. He did not try to stop her. All believers should seek to live the life that is <u>acceptable</u> to the Lord. The Bible says, "Let the words of my mouth, and the meditation of my heart, be acceptable in Thy sight, O LORD, my strength, and my redeemer." Psalm 19:14.

What we say, and our heart's desire should always please the Lord.

"The lips of the righteous know what is <u>acceptable</u>: but the mouth of the wicked speaketh frowardness." Proverbs 10:32.

Often, we allow our words to dishonor the Lord and sometimes even discourage others (Proverbs 18:21).

★ ★ ★ ★ ★ 45

We should give our lives to the things that are <u>acceptable</u> to God.

"I beseech you therefore, brethren, by the mercies of God, that ye present your bodies a living sacrifice, holy, acceptable unto God, which is your reasonable service. And be not conformed to this world: but be ye transformed by the renewing of your mind, that ye may prove what is that good, and <u>acceptable</u>, and perfect, will of God." Romans 12:1-2.

"Proving what is acceptable unto the Lord." Ephesians 5:10, Paul said, "But I have all, and abound: I am full, having received of Epaphroditus the things which were sent from you, an odour of a sweet smell, a sacrifice acceptable, well pleasing to God." Philippians 4:18.

Mary had given herself to the Lord and wanted to please Him with her life. Have we given ourselves to the Lord, and are we seeking to please Him with our lives?

He Appraised It
Jesus said, "She hath done what she could…" Mark 14:8.

Some have suggested that this ointment was worth a man's wage for an entire year or a woman's wage for three years. It was all she had. It was all she could do. Many will live and never do what they could do for the Lord. Mary had the joy of knowing that she did what she could.

I have heard people say, "When I retire, I'll do more for the Lord," or "When I am financially established, I'll do more for

★ ★ ★ ★ ★

the Lord." Why wait until the end of your life to do something for the Lord? Why do so many only want to give the Lord the leftovers?

Will the Lord be able to say to us that we have done what we could?

He Anointed It
"Verily I say unto you, Wheresoever this gospel shall be preached throughout the whole world, this also that she hath done shall be spoken of for a memorial of her." Mark 14:9.

The Lord Jesus used this to teach a great truth of Calvary and His sacrifice. On Calvary He would be broken and poured out. Sitting at this table was a great object lesson. On one side was Lazarus which had been dead; on the other was Simon, which was a leper but now is cleansed. Calvary is not only a place to receive life and to be born again; it is a place where the child of God can go for cleansing.

God allowed Mary to see the Lord, and on one side a lost sinner, and on the other a child of God who needed cleansing.

The ointment represents the blood shed for all. Calvary was not a waste. God did not measure a little of His love; He poured it all out at Calvary. The Lord used Mary's act of love to teach the great truth of His sacrifice for us.

The question to consider is, 'Who put in the heart of Mary to do what she did?' The answer is in an unusual statement

★ ★ ★ ★ ★   47

God puts in our text. The Bible says, "When Jesus understood it." Wow!

Jesus understood that this was something God put in the heart of Mary to do. Remember these are the final days of the Lord Jesus' earthly ministry. He has tried to prepare His followers for His impending death.

But, so far, every time He has tried to tell them, someone says something to change the subject.

The Bible says, "Peter took him," (Jesus) "and began to rebuke him, saying, Be it far from thee, Lord: this shall not be unto thee. But he" (Jesus) "turned, and said unto Peter, Get thee behind me, Satan: thou art an offence unto me: for thou savourest not the things that be of God, but those that be of men." Mathew 16:22-23.

The next time Jesus tried to prepare His followers for His death on Calvary, the mother of James and John asked Jesus a question. "She saith unto him, Grant that these my two sons may sit, the one on thy right hand, and the other on the left, in thy kingdom." Matthew 20:21.

No one interrupted Jesus this time. He used what Mary did as an object lesson explaining His dying for our sin. God put it in the heart of Mary to do what she did. God always puts what He wants done, in this world, in the hearts of His people. Nehemiah said, "neither told I *any* man what my God had put in my heart to..." Nehemiah 2:12.

★ ★ ★ ★ ★

Questions to consider.

- What is acceptable and what is not acceptable to the Lord in our lives?

- How do we measure our gifts and dedication to Christ? (By what is left?)

- What has the Lord put in your heart to do?

Lesson #4
MARY'S HEAVENLY REWARD

"Jesus said, Let her alone; why trouble ye her? she hath wrought a good work on Me. For ye have the poor with you always, and whensoever ye will ye may do them good: but Me ye have not always.

She hath done what she could: she is come aforehand to anoint My body to the burying. Verily I say unto you, <u>Wheresoever this gospel shall be preached throughout the whole world, this also that she hath done shall be spoken of for a memorial of her</u>." Mark 14:6-9.

So far, we have answered several questions about Mary and her Alabaster box.

- **We know what Mary did that was so blessed.** Mary according to Jesus, "wrought a good work on Me… She hath done what she could."

- **We know when she did it.** Mary did this at the closing of the Lord Jesus' earthly ministry. Jesus said, "she is come aforehand to anoint My body to the burying."

- **We know where it was done.** Everyone was together "in Bethany in the house of Simon the leper, as he sat at meat" and "Lazarus was one of them that sat at the table with him." Mark 14:3, John 12:2.

- **We know why Mary did it.** God put it in her heart to do. Ezra said, "Blessed be the LORD God of our fathers, which hath put such a thing as this in the…heart." Ezra 7:27.

- **We know how the Lord Jesus used it.** The Lord used it to illustrate His dying for our sins. "And there were some that had indignation within themselves, and said, Why was this waste of the ointment made?" Mark 14:4.

MARY'S HEAVENLY REWARD

Mary was not concerned about her reward when she gave her ointment to the Lord Jesus. Her only concern was that she did what was in her heart to do.

True servants of the Lord are not in it for the reward. They serve the Lord because they love Him "For the love of Christ constraineth us; because we thus judge, that if one died for all, then were all dead." II Corinthians 5:14.

God puts His will in the hearts of His children.

God puts what He wants done, in this world, in the hearts of His children. We see this truth taught in the Bible.

Nehemiah said about what God put in his heart. He said, "And I arose in the night, I and some few men with me; neither told I *any* man what my God had put in my heart to do at Jerusalem." Nehemiah 2:12.

★ ★ ★ ★ ★

It is **important** to understand that God put in Mary's heart what she did for Jesus.

However, it is **more important** to understand why the Lord Jesus wanted His followers to invest what Mary did.

But, the **most important** truth we glean from Mary's act of love and kindness is to see that her memorial (reward) is not finished until the trumpet sounds.

Doing God's will brings treasures in Heaven.

Mary's reward is her treasures in Heaven. When Jesus told His followers to tell what Mary did, He made sure Mary's investment would never be forgotten. Mary's reward is yet to be seen; because a gift given in God's work is an investment that keeps growing and growing with every generation. Mary's reward is yet to be seen.

What makes Mary's reward different is what Jesus said about what she did. He said, "<u>Wheresoever this gospel shall be preached throughout the whole world, this also that she hath done shall be spoken of for a memorial of her.</u>"

In other words, everyone who preaches or teaches the Bible, is to make sure they tell what Mary did for Him on this day.

The Bible says, "For we must all appear before the judgment seat of Christ; that every one may receive the things done in his body, according to that he hath done, whether it be good or bad." II Corinthians 5:10.

★ ★ ★ ★ ★

The Judgment seat of Christ is the time when all that has been done for the Gospel will be revealed and rewarded. Mary's reward will be revealed that day.

After two thousand years of reinvesting what she did, one can only imagine what the Judgement Seat of Christ has in store for her.

Our greatest reward will come from our influence.

Our greatest reward, at the Judgement seat of Christ, will come because of our influence from generation to generation. The Bible says, "For none of us liveth to himself, and no man dieth to himself." Romans 14:7. All believers' lives and influence is to be carried forward from faith to faith. Influence lives beyond the grave good or bad.

This is why Paul told the followers in Philippi to continue, "Holding forth the word of life; that I may rejoice in the day of Christ, that I have not run in vain, neither laboured in vain." Philippians 2:16.

Paul understood how every life, moving forward, must stay connected to the past; and that every believer needs to reinvest the lives that were invested in them.

Mary's gift and actions were not just about money and monetary worth, but it was about the lives that touched her life. What we give as our "Alabaster Gift" should reflect every life that made our life.

★ ★ ★ ★ ★

We give not only because of what Jesus means to us, but because of what others have also meant to us. We give in memory.

Jesus said, "Whosoever will come after me, let him deny himself, and take up his cross, and follow me. For whosoever will save his life shall lose it; but whosoever shall lose his life for my sake and the gospel's, the same shall save it." Mark 8:34-35.

Our life's reward reaches back to the day of our salvation unto the day we depart this world. What determines our reward for our labor is how we invested what was given to us. Remember, to whom much is given much is required. Our greatest reward will be determined if we do something eternal with our influence.

Did we reinvest the lives of the people who invested their life in us? Did we give beyond our finances? How many people were strengthened because we lived? Did we leave behind something that will live to the end of time; something worthy for the Judgement Seat of Christ.

Our life's work is being recorded.

Believers have a book of their lives kept in Heaven, and one day we will see it. The Bible speaks about that book when David said, "Thou tellest my wanderings: put thou my tears into thy bottle: are they not in thy book?" Psalms 56:8.

The Lord does not let any act of kindness or love go unnoticed. He keeps a very good record, and one day He will reward us.

Jesus said, "And whosoever shall give to drink unto one of these little ones a cup of cold water only in the name of a disciple, verily I say unto you, he shall in no wise lose his reward." Matthew 10:42.

Our reward will be our treasures in Heaven. Jesus said, "Lay not up for yourselves treasures upon earth, where moth and rust doth corrupt, and where thieves break through and steal:

But lay up for yourselves <u>treasures in heaven</u>, where neither moth nor rust doth corrupt, and where thieves do not break through nor steal: For where your treasure is, there will your heart be also." Matthew 6:19-21.

Paul, in writing to the first century believers, challenged them by saying, "Holding forth the word of life; that I may rejoice in the day of Christ, that I have not run in vain, neither laboured in vain." Philippians 2:16.

Here is how it works. People, who invested in our life, will be rejoicing to see what their life's investment produced in God's work through us, if we are "Holding forth the word of life."

Think what it will be like seeing all who carried forward the teachings of Jesus and who continued in the Apostles doc-

★ ★ ★ ★ ★

trine, as the Lord works back through human history until the first century Christians.

This truth is illustrated in the parable of the laborers, as taught by Jesus.

What Paul writes to the believers in Philippi helps us to understand that at the Rapture, the last person saved will be the first ones to the Judgement Seat of Christ. Then we will work our way back through human history from generation to generation. Everyone will see what they carried forward, and what they left behind.

Then we will see how we are all connected and that there is nothing new under the sun. One life touched another life, then that life touched a new life, and so on, and so forth, until we were reached. The question we must ask is, "Will the connection continue or end with our generation?"

Determine not to let the spreading of the Gospel worldwide end with you and your generation.

Every generation must have followers of Christ who are willing to break their "Alabaster Box" for the Gospel. Join the brotherhood and sisterhood of the Alabaster Box.

David told us about a man in his generation who gave to a king like a king giveth to another king. (II Samuel 24:24)

★ ★ ★ ★ ★

Questions to consider.

- Are you thankful for all the generations of believers who made your life possible?

- Do you want to join the fellowship of the Alabaster Box breakers?

- What would make your gift worthy of a King?

God put in Mary's heart to do what she did.

Mary, bringing her Alabaster box and pouring it on Jesus, is another example of how God the Father was working with Jesus during His earthly mission. It was God who put in Mary's heart to do what she did that day. God put something in Mary's heart to do for Jesus, and she did it!

I have always stopped and listened very carefully when a Christian says, "God has put something in my heart to do for the Lord." I understand God puts everything He wants done in this world into the hearts of His followers.

I have given my life to help practicing Christians do what God has put in their heart to do. The question I have for you is, "What has God put in your heart to do with your life and treasures for Him?"

"Only one Life 'Twill soon be past.

Only what's done For Christ will Last." Missionary C. T. Studd 1860-1931.

★ ★ ★ ★ ★

Pour it on Jesus

★ ★ ★ ★ ★

— SECTION THREE —

Pour it on Jesus

Breaking
Your Alabaster Box

Student
Lessons

★ ★ ★ ★ ★

Pour It On Jesus
Song

Student Lessons

MARY'S REASON FOR POURING IT ON JESUS

THE CROWD'S REACTION TO MARY'S GIFT

THE LORD'S RESPONSE TO MARY'S GIFT

MARY'S HEAVENLY REWARD

Dr. Tom Sexton

★ ★ ★ ★ ★

Pour It on Jesus
Sung to the tune of "Tell It To Jesus"

Have you trusted Christ's work of redemption?
Pour it on Jesus, pour it on Jesus.
Do you know Him as your Lord and Saviour?
Pour it on Jesus today.

CHORUS

Have you loved ones lost in their sin?
Pour it on Jesus, pour it on Jesus.
There's no other who can redeem them.
Pour it on Jesus today.

CHORUS

There are others waiting on the message.
Pour it on Jesus, pour it on Jesus.
The devil's kingdom can be defeated!
Pour it on Jesus today.

CHORUS

Do you long for treasures up in heaven?
Pour it on Jesus, pour it on Jesus.
Then you must make an investment.
Pour it on Jesus today.

CHORUS

Pour it on Jesus, pour it on Jesus.
There is no gift that's a waste.
He's our Saviour and He has redeemed us.
Pour it on Jesus today.

★ ★ ★ ★ ★

Student Lesson #1
MARY'S REASON FOR POURING IT ON JESUS

"There they made Him a supper; and Martha served: but Lazarus was one of them that sat at the table with Him.

Then took Mary a pound of ointment of spikenard, very costly, and anointed the feet of Jesus, and wiped His feet with her hair: and the house was filled with the odour of the ointment." John 12:2-11.

Mary Broke Her Alabaster Box
First, because of what Jesus had done for her.

"Jesus saith unto her, Said I not unto thee, that, if thou wouldest believe, thou shouldest see the glory of God...Salvation is of the LORD." John 11:40. "And you hath he quickened, who were dead in trespasses and sins;" Ephesians 2:1.

Mary Broke Her Alabaster Box
Second, because of what Jesus has done for her family.

"And when he thus had spoken, he cried with a loud voice, <u>Lazarus, come forth</u>. And he that was dead came forth, bound hand and foot with graveclothes: and his face was bound about with a napkin. Jesus saith unto them, Loose him, and let him go." John 11:43-44.

★ ★ ★ ★ ★

Mary Broke Her Alabaster Box
Third, because of what Jesus has done for her friends and neighbors.

"Then <u>many of the Jews</u> which came to Mary, and had seen the things which Jesus did, <u>believed on him</u>." John 11:45.

Questions to consider.

- How has the Lord strengthened your faith?

- How has God helped you see a bigger picture of what He is doing?

- Have you seen the Lord work in your friends and neighbor's lives?

★ ★ ★ ★ ★

Student Lesson #2
THE CROWD'S REACTION TO MARY'S GIFT

"And being in Bethany in the house of Simon the leper, as He sat at meat, there came a woman having an alabaster box of ointment of spikenard very precious; and she break the box and poured it on His head…. And they murmured against her." Mark 14:3-9, vv. 3-5.

The Bible says that "…they murmured against her." These three groups represent the three groups that are in our churches. All of us will find ourselves in one of these three groups.

Some Thought Nothing Should Been Done

"Then saith one of His disciples, Judas Iscariot, Simon's son, which should betray Him, Why was not this ointment sold for three hundred pence, and given to the poor? This he said, not that he cared for the poor…" John 12:4-6.

Some Thought It Should Have Been Measured Out, Not Poured Out

"There came unto Him a woman having an alabaster box of very precious ointment, and poured it on His head…<u>But when His disciples saw it, they had indignation</u>, saying, To what purpose is this waste?" Matthew 26:7-8.

Some Believed It Should Be All Poured Out On Jesus

"And there were <u>some</u> that had indignation." Mark 14:4. Mark's Gospel says "some," not all. There were some who believed it should be poured out. There were at least two other people sitting at the table with Jesus. This group is represented by Simon, the person with leprosy, and Lazarus.

Questions to consider.

- Are there people in our churches who do nothing for the Lord? For example, they do not give, serve in the ministry, or invite others to church.

- Are there those in our churches who do only what is required? For example, they give exactly 10% to the penny in giving the tithe. They do the minimum in service or church attendance.

- Are there those in our churches who hold back nothing? In their giving and Christian service, they find ways to pour out their lives to Christ.

The big question is, "What group do you want to be in?"

★ ★ ★ ★ ★

Student Lesson #3
THE LORD'S RESPONSE TO MARY'S GIFT

"<u>And Jesus said, Let her alone; why trouble ye her? she hath wrought a good work on Me.</u> For ye have the poor with you always, and whensoever ye will ye may do them good: but Me ye have not always. <u>She hath done what she could</u>: she is come aforehand to anoint My body to the burying.

He Accepted It
Jesus said, "Let her alone…why trouble ye her…
She hath wrought a good work on Me." Mark 14:6.

The Lord Jesus accepted Mary's act of love and kindness. He did not try to stop her. All believers should seek to live the life that is acceptable to the Lord. The Bible says, "Let the words of my mouth, and the meditation of my heart, be acceptable in Thy sight, O LORD, my strength, and my redeemer." Psalm 19:14.

He Appraised It
Jesus said, "She hath done what she could…" Mark 14:8.

Some have suggested that this ointment was worth a man's wage for an entire year or a woman's wage for three years. It was all she had. It was all she could do. Many will live and never do what they could do for the Lord. Mary had the joy of knowing that she did what she could.

★ ★ ★ ★ ★

He Anointed It

"Verily I say unto you, Wheresoever this gospel shall be preached throughout the whole world, this also that she hath done shall be spoken of for a memorial of her." Mark 14:9.

The Lord Jesus used this to teach a great truth of Calvary and His sacrifice. On Calvary He would be broken and poured out. Sitting at this table was a great object lesson. On one side was Lazarus which had been dead; on the other was Simon, which was a leper but now is cleansed. Calvary is not only a place to receive life and to be born again; it is a place where the child of God can go for cleansing.

Questions to consider.

- What is acceptable and what is not acceptable to the Lord in our lives?

- How do we measure our gifts and dedication to Christ? (By what is left?)

- What has the Lord put in your heart to do?

★ ★ ★ ★ ★

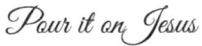

Student Lesson #4
MARY'S HEAVENLY REWARD

"Jesus said, Let her alone; why trouble ye her? she hath wrought a good work on Me. For ye have the poor with you always, and whensoever ye will ye may do them good: but Me ye have not always.

She hath done what she could: she is come aforehand to anoint My body to the burying. Verily I say unto you, <u>Wheresoever this gospel shall be preached throughout the whole world, this also that she hath done shall be spoken of for a memorial of her</u>." Mark 14:6-9.

Mary was not concerned about her reward when she gave her ointment to the Lord Jesus. Her only concern was that she did what was in her heart to do.

God puts His will in the hearts of His children.

God puts what He wants done, in this world, in the hearts of His children. We see this truth taught in the Bible.

Nehemiah said about what God put in his heart. He said, "And I arose in the night, I and some few men with me; neither told I *any* man what my God had put in my heart to do at Jerusalem." Nehemiah 2:12.

★ ★ ★ ★ ★

Doing God's will brings treasures in Heaven.

Mary's reward is her treasures in Heaven. When Jesus told His followers to tell what Mary did, He made sure Mary's investment would never be forgotten. Mary's reward is yet to be seen; because a gift given in God's work is an investment that keeps growing and growing with every generation. Mary's reward is yet to be seen.

Our life's work is being recorded.

Believers have a book of their lives kept in Heaven, and one day we will see it. The Bible speaks about that book when David said, "Thou tellest my wanderings: put thou my tears into thy bottle: are they not in thy book?" Psalms 56:8.

Questions to consider.

- Are you thankful for all the generations of believers who made your life possible?

- Do you want to join the fellowship of the Alabaster Box breakers?

- What would make your gift worthy of a King?

★ ★ ★ ★ ★   69

★ ★ ★ ★ ★

BREAKING THE ALABASTER BOX
Getting the Most Out of This Campaign

1. Ask the LORD to open people's minds and hearts of understanding about giving.

2. Use all the material that is provided by Five Star Christian Ministries. www.FiveStarChristianMinistries.com

   It is important that each teacher have all the material. Teachers will need to read over all the material and be familiar with each lesson. Ask each teacher to read this book.

3. Set a date for a "Breaking Your Alabaster Box."

   Make sure it is a day when people will be in town (not a holiday weekend). Do not have it before people get paid, if their checks come in on the first of the month, etc.

4. Get everyone involved: bus routes, Sunday School classes, etc.

5. Set a goal and make it public.

6. Tell people what the "Pour It On Jesus Offering" will be used for.

★ ★ ★ ★ ★

Pour it on Jesus

★ ★ ★ ★ ★

ARE YOU GOING TO HEAVEN
Jesus Wants Your Forever to be lived In Heaven

God loves you. The Bible says, "For God so loved the world, that he gave his only begotten Son, that whosoever believeth in him should not perish, but have everlasting life." John 3: 16.

This great Bible verse reveals four truths from the heart of Jesus for all people.

Jesus Said We Are Loved.

Jesus said, "For God so loved the world…." You are a part of this world, and God loves you. He gave His Son for you, and He wants you "…to know the love of Christ…" Ephesians 3:19.

Jesus Said We Are of Worth.

Jesus wants us to know that **we are of worth**. We are so dear to God "…that He gave His only begotten Son…." The Bible teaches us that we are all sinners, "For all have sinned, and come short of the glory of God" Romans 3:23

Our sin must be paid for. "For the wages of sin is death…" Romans 6:23.

★ ★ ★ ★ ★   73

Jesus "died for our sins according to the scriptures" I Corinthians 15:3. God demonstrated His love for us and our worth to Him when He sent His Son to die in our place.

You may ask, "How can God forgive **my** sin?" He can because of what Jesus did. "…While we were yet sinners, Christ died for us." Romans 5:8.

Jesus Said We Can Have Hope.

God wants us to know that **we can have hope**. Jesus said, "…that whosoever believeth in Him should not perish…."

Life is fragile, and people are perishing. Jesus said I came "…that they might have life, and that they might have it more abundantly." John 10:10.

In a world where so many have lost hope, God wants us to know that the "…Lord Jesus Christ…is our hope." I Timothy 1:1.

He rose from the dead, and He said, "…Because **I** live, **ye** shall live also." John 14:19.

Jesus Said Our Life Can Have Purpose.

Jesus wants us to know that **we can have purpose** in life. He desires that we "…should not perish but have everlasting life." "And this is the promise that He hath promised us, even eternal life." I John 2:25. You may ask,

"How can **I** receive God's promise of eternal life?"

Acknowledge that you are a sinner, "for all have sinned, and come short of the glory of God." Romans 3:23.

Believe that the Lord Jesus died for you, "Christ died for our sins according to the scriptures." I Corinthians 15:3.

Call upon the Lord to save you, "for whosoever shall call upon the name of the Lord shall be saved." Romans 10:13.

If you would be willing to turn to Christ in repentance and faith, pray this simple prayer of salvation:

"Lord Jesus, I know that I am a sinner, and I believe You died and rose again for me. I trust You to forgive me and deliver me from my sin. Come into my heart and save me. Help me to live for You. Amen."

Jesus said, "...I give unto them eternal life; and they shall never perish..." John 10:28.

Everlasting life is ours when we receive Christ as our personal Saviour. God bless you.

★ ★ ★ ★ ★

For more helpful information visit
www.FiveStarChristianMinistries.com

www.ingramcontent.com/pod-product-compliance
Lightning Source LLC
Chambersburg PA
CBHW051550120626
46551CB00013B/1444